To Touch Your Heart

Christine J. Logan

Library and Archives Canada Cataloguing in Publication

Logan, Christine J., 1964-
To touch your heart : poems of inspiration / Christine J.
Logan.
ISBN 978-0-9869229-0-9
I. Title.
PS8623.O36T68 2011 C811'.6 C2011-902577-9

Contents

With special love for my daughter
Mary Margaret

Christine J. Logan

Acknowledgements

I wish to thank Jim Bisacowski from Book Design and Melody Poirier from Island Blue Print for helping me make this book possible and my goal come true.

This book has taken me 31 years to write. I was 15years old when I wrote my first 3 poems. I have been blessed with the courage to put my thoughts on paper, to be able to share my thoughts and imagination with you.

Heartfelt thanks are sent to my beautiful daughter, Mary. Thank you for all your support and encouragement.

I wish to thank all of you who have inspired me over the years. If it were not for you touching my heart, This book of poems would only be thoughts.

Bless you all!

Mary

My eyes see you
With a smile so modest
With your heart so big

My eyes see you
Care so deeply
With your feelings overflowing

My eyes see you
Growing so lovely
With your beauty

I love you.

Mission Tree

Mission tree, wait for me
To say hello
To see you stand alone
So full and round

The drive toward your home
Your field
Where you live

Inspires me to smile
Before I even see you

Mission tree
My favourite tree.

Smile for me

As the sun shines on your smile
We walk side by side a while

Hands linked with passion
In a traditional, old style fashion
Through tall and mysterious trees
We kick and play among the crunchy leaves

Our hearts communicate
To stop and kiss on a dime

The racing and beating
And pumping inside us

Reminds us
To value and savour our time.

Heart's Wishes

You're my heart's wishes
My dream's kisses

You're my star's sparkle
My apple's pie

Can't forget the twinkle in your eye

You're the cat's meow
I wonder now
How we'll find each other as one

Hmmmm...nice thought!

  Christine J. Logan

Snowy Days

This year's snow is abundant
Be like-mind of a child
Have fun in it

To walk through knee-high seas of snow
Is more of an adventure
Than you will know

The glimmer on its surface
Delightful and bright
Is the same as the smile I get
In just the right light
Let your heart and body return to play
Enjoy your freedom in a wondrous day

This kind of snowfall is a blessing to those
Who make the most of what weather throws

Remember, this kind of love and child-like ways
Comes from within on snowy days.

Love

She lives her life with much joy and care
To be of this mind is easy to share

She cherishes memories of the past
With much love to give
Love that lasts

She chooses one man to share her dreams
His name is Al, together their love
Will sail through plenty of streams

Our Father knows when the time is right
She will be blessed on that glorious night

Two hearts unite and share their love
She, her man and their Father above.

Waiting's ok

Waiting is easy
When you're filled with joy
When you're not in a hurry
Or haven't a ploy

It's different than having patience you know
It's amazing and kind
When it's love that you hold

Patience is sometimes often quite hard
So turn it to waiting
It changes your heart.

Jump!

Jump! On your bed so high
You'll get in trouble or hurt and cry

Jump! Start your car and thank a stranger
It's what his cables were paid for

Jump! In the deep end and swim around
Live life on the edge and lose that frown

Jump! Up and down, shake off the rust
Life is short
Live it or bust!

Dusty

Though we're far apart
Our days we must consume

For every passing moment
In my heart and soul,
For you, is room

You fill my thoughts
When we're apart
When you're home
You warm my heart

Missing you is often hard
I close my eyes
And count the days

And when you're home,
I scream...

Yayyy!!

Dusty on the Road

Dusty moves
With the sky we share
Rolling along the highway
No time to spare

Dusty knows
His sweetness will wait
Each gathering moment
Together, it's great

Dusty's so smooth
So cool
So real
He's gone a short while
Then home with appeal.

 Christine J. Logan

Dusty's Home

There's a race to the door
As footsteps they hear

Up the back stairs
His girls would cheer

Kisses and hugs could never compare
With the love and happiness
Of his return.

True Treasures

Love given to those you care for
Moments too silly to forget
Fresh air so wet and clean
From a hot day's first rain

Thumb wrestling to bypass time
Kissing without rhyme

Forests so green and alive
With wildlife noises
And then... quiet too

More than time itself
I love you and you and you!

Charlie Power

Charlene
Chuck for short

Power and love
Deep inside
Released slow and sure

Friends for life
Sisters too

Our love grows constantly
With time and strengthens pure

Chuck & Dino
Silly for sure!

My Happiness Within

My happiness overflows
With the tune of a favourite song

The smell of good cologne
The strength of a hug
The warmth of a gentle touch

The taste of smooth chocolate
Passion from the one you love

The contagious joy in a smile
Memories
Today and tomorrow to come.

Whose Eyes are These ?

Whose eyes are these
I can not tell
Surrounded by the night

Intense and curious
Found a-glow
Lost only in my headlights

Serious eyes
Lost in thought or
Happy eyes
Whose trail's alive and hot

Eyes of the aged
Waiting to tell stories
Of a lifetime
Passed onto eager ears anxious to listen

Or puppy eyes
Looking up with
Unconditional love
Hopeful response and glisten

Whose eyes are these
But one racoon
Finding his way home
To his sweetie to spoon.

To Touch

To touch is as sweet
As a baby's first cuddle

To touch is as cool
As a walk on a crisp, spring eve

To touch is as fiery
As the passion
From a luscious lover

To touch is to feel
To feel is to care
To care is to love
And to love is to be happy.

This Christmas Season

This Christmas season, I believe in...
    The hope we all have inside us
    The faith we should have and
    The love for others we could have

This Christmas season, I have a reason...
    To hold my head up strong
    To love the world of all who live it
    And forgive those who've done wrong

This Christmas season, is amazing...
    To know I am loved and held dear
    To those around me and God above
    Who walks with me through with
    His guiding love

This Christmas, to all, my one true wish...
    Is to give of yourselves to those in need
    And pray and love and spread good deeds

This Christmas to you, I wish the best...
    Happy New Year and to all
    Be blessed!

Rest Assured

To this our day
We try our best

Among our struggles
We will not rest

Until this time
Our day is done

We say goodnight
Unto the sun.

God

For the love of God has touched in me
When born and when I die

For the love of God, for Who I pray upon
When confused and when I cry

For the love of God, Who is with me always
And forever, wherever I may wonder

For the love of God is true and very great
No matter who He looks upon or why

I shall never stop loving
The ones I love.

(written at age 15)

Everyday

To those who walk upon the streets
When dark or when light
They shall always remember that
Every day may or may not be the same

So those who know how their every day
Is going to turn out
Have something to look forward to
And look towards and upon

Lo as it may seem if your every day is so
You have dreams to imagine
How your future will improve.

(written at age 15)

For Those with Love

For those who come into my life are real
And those who are real are beautiful

For those who love me and are to be loved
Are kindly generous and acceptable

For those who wish to live a lifetime
Have an extra exciting life to live

For those who care, not only for themselves
But for others, they are who I love
And appreciate
For those who accept what is given unto
Are able to give back with more love

For all who live and love
In their own special way
Have their own thoughts
And love to give and receive
From beautiful people who
Think the way I was made to think.

(written at age 15)

Love's Kiss

True love's kiss
Comes to you
With love and adoration

Receive this gift
From your true love
With lasting admiration.

In The Light

A poem is about to unfold
Before your ears it will be told

It's about a girl born anew
To the Father, through the Son

His Holy Spirit will live within
To unite their love, to repel all sin

She learns and grows every day
To exciting knowledge along the way

The words of her Father she reads
With thanks and praise, she gives

Her way is marked by her Father's Light
So she may never fall out of sight

She thanks the Lord and holds the hand
With the Holy Spirit, which comes to her
From her Father... Greatest of All !

Moms

As for moms
I am one too
I teach my daughter to be true

My love for moms has grown
From the moment I've known you, Yvonne

Don't get me wrong
I love my mom too
My heart tells me
I have two!

Things For Sure

Pages with words
Feelings and thoughts
Put them together
Poetry, it can be saved, it can be bought

Imagination, colors and shades
Paper and a brush
To each his own, alike or not
A frame with a home
Will find the perfect spot

A look, a glance
First kisses, more
Time will tell what's in store

What's meant to be, will be
So take your time, never rush
And you will look back
With thoughts of love.

Two Uncles

Two uncles I admire
Two uncles and their kin

Two uncles hold my gratitude
And all my love within

Two uncles I cherish
Two uncles so fine
Two uncles with their tales so tall
I'm so very happy they are mine

Two uncles you would love to know
Two uncles sure and true

Two uncles hold a lot of hearts
Two uncles, I can assure you

If I did not know them
My heart would sure be blue.

My Purpose

I know there is a purpose
There just has to be
My heart has traveled many places
With only myself to remember my traces

I'm certain there must be a purpose for me
Until the day I know for sure
I'll test the waters of my future

A little fun, a little scary
In my past, I found a path
That brought me my Mary

My future comes to me day by day
My heart holds strong
With uncertain steps along the way

My faith holds me tight
With patience and love
To guide me to my purpose above.

Where Does it End?

Where does it end
What do we know
How far do we travel
How long is this show

It seems ok, it seems just fine
To know this story is about me
To know that it is mine

Sometimes I laugh
Sometimes I cry
Sometimes I just don't know why

It only seems to me, it must come out
For I am not the person to whom must shout

I have many questions
Many doubts too
Many content moments
And many concerned friends

I think it's all behind me
I think it's becoming clear

To find the road I travel on
Is always very near.

  Christine J. Logan

If Love Were Like Ice Cream

If love were like ice cream
Life would be grand

My love for all in this world
Like flavours of ice cream
Limitless, in the palm of your hand

If love were like ice cream
You would be tops
Covered in sprinkles
That never runs out

If love were like ice cream
Every day would be hot
I'd pick any flavour
Now that hit the spot

The flavours are endless
So is the love
Hand in hand together
They fit like a glove

If love were like ice cream
All flavours tried
They would all come in second
When it comes to loving you!

If Only

If only we knew what was next
Life would be too easy

The uncertain fear of what was to come
Would simply be a matter of what once was

A step of life we risk to take
A hope for change and fun

If only our souls were whole to start with
This journey would save us grief

We live our lives, love our mankind
And eat way too much beef

If only life was easy
If only we all held hands

This world would be a happier place
And we would all be friends.

Thanks and Blessings

I pray this to our Father
And thank Him every day
For His guidance and His will
I'm in Your arms to stay

I pray to God
Have fear no longer
Hold tight our hearts
Have faith, grow stronger

I pray His blessings be on us
To see us through hard times
To share love and understanding
On our lives' path of dimes.

Holdfast My Love

This ride is swift but sweet, my dear
The hours glide so fast
Our hearts know no limit of this
Time freezes at our stand
Counting down to our next round
Only defeats the purpose
When we are two people, we are just one
And life goes on around us

Our love surpasses all
And rings on that bell
With the speed of light
And all that comes with it
Time will stand still

Holdfast my love
We have a wondrous, long journey
Ahead of us.

Freedom

In my lap lay a kitten
No fear is known

The nudge of her nose
When I lean in to kiss
Is a treasure I would certainly miss

For the second I move
Or flinch a brow

She'll no longer be
Under my gentle hand

I'll stand up straight
And shake off my lap
Only to find her at my feet
Taking a nap!

Fear or Faith

Some dark paths still linger
In the far, back corner of my mind

My heart tells me not to worry
Pay no attention to that tear in my eye

God is very close indeed
With His loving Son to show me how
To hand Him over all my fears
And dance in His glory with no doubts

Thank You, Lord, for all Your blessings
For without You, I would not have found
That faith stands strong
And fear holds no bounds.

In My Eyes

In my eyes, you will not see
No hate, no fear, no doubt from me

The Lord has blessed me
With love and joy
To share with others with hope and belief

In my eyes, you will not see
No anger, no spite, no jealousy

You will find a light, a smile
A way within, to hold your hope
And let your journey begin

In my eyes, you will see
When I trust the Lord and believe
Nothing is forsaken me.

Listen

Listen to your inner self
It's always right
Believe it or not, it comes from God
It is a gift, it is your sight

Listen to the choices in your mind
There's a right and a wrong
A why should I and a why should I not

Choose the answer that comes from within
The path you pick will bring salvation

Listen, with long term results
Knowing you're never alone
Will comfort your heart
Listen now, listen with truth
Your future on earth and in heaven
Is all up to you.

  Christine J. Logan

This Day Comes

This day comes when we awake
With actions, words and steps we take

To be as He, kind and good
With thoughts of love and hopes
Of our lives understood

It's only we that think this small
To carry on with no thought at all
Of what's in store and what's ahead

We have no idea
Until this day comes.

Not Ourselves

This life, we're only borrowing it
It is not ours to keep

It belongs to this world
It belongs to the past
It has an end, it will not last

Our souls, however, if we believe
In Whom He is and what He's done
Will change us all and last forever

Do not forget, we are His
And He is ours
Look past yourselves
And shoot for the stars.

On Guard

On guard for those we love
We keep an open eye

We see the wrong and stay away
Teach what we know
And what we can
For those we wish to pray

Love is strong, it will not break
When two are one for Heaven's sake

They bind together, their love of God
And pray for others
To stay on guard.

Silly Aunt Millie

I'm just a wishy, girly girl
Who loves to be so silly

Pull up some grass and sit on your
......bottom

I'll tell you a story about my
Aunt Millie

She told me once, to act my age
When grown-ups were around

But in her case, she told me twice
In her could not be found

She had to laugh, she had to be silly
She said she was three years old
Trapped inside a silly, old Aunt Millie.

  Christine J. Logan

This Love

This day begins
When I awake

I will not think twice
I will not forsake

All is blessed
With the Spirit of Love

This love is seen
In all we do
It fills in me
It can fill in you.

Holy Smokes ? <3 ! :)

Holy smokes
I can't believe it

Oh my gosh
Is it really true

Get out
You've got to be kidding

For real
No way

Unbelievable
Wow

Is that really you

One

One, in a glance
Filled with romance

One, in a gentle touch
Too much is never too much

One, for each other
From lover to lover

One, where hearts bond
No words need spoken

One, unconditional love
Never broken.

Your Hands

Your hands guide me
So I don't lose sight
Of what is good and what is right
Your gentle nudge
Lets me know
How much You care with what You show

The lessons that I live through
Teach me to be true
To share Your love with others
In hopes they'll love You too

The reason that I seek You
The reason that I care
Is simply based upon one word, "Love"
It's love I need from You
It's love I need to share

So, with Your love and grace on me
Guide me to all others
And when it comes right down to it
I pray for this, for You

In all the heaven and all the lands
I pray their souls be in Your hands.

  Christine J. Logan

Be Good

I once had a dream
Where a man had been shot

Two seconds later
The man who shot him also died

He tested good
And deserved what he got

I stood there
Holding my own death papers
Hearing a voice
I heard this said

Maybe you're dreaming
You have a gift
You're not really dead.

One Step Ahead

Bad dreams and doubts
Negative thoughts and words

Can all be forgiven
If you carry His sword

His sword is to protect you
From evil and sin

Cover yourself with the shield
From within

Trust not what you can do for yourself
But for others instead

Follow this rule
And the Holy Spirit will keep you
One step ahead.

Memories

Once I sat nude in the mud
When I was just a babe

The touch of rich soil
The scent of the dirt
When it first starts to rain

Has stayed with me
All of my life
And will never go away

My mama taught me
Just before it rains
You feel the moisture in the air
And the smell of damp soil
Is everywhere

Today, you won't find me
Nude in the mud
But thankful for memories
And my mom.

Let Him In

We can open the door
And let Him in

He can open our hearts
Transform our thinking
Love will dwell within

Our love for others
Will continue to grow
As we learn from the Son

Our Father in heaven
We then shall know.

My Girl

I have a girl
She's all grown up

I beam inside
Just thinking about her

I dream at night
She is so young
Maybe six or maybe nine

She sings so sweet
She's so content

I feel so blessed
I thank You, God

For sending me my daughter
For sending me a friend.

Follow Your Feet

This is it!
It's what your dealt
What do you want to do

Listen to your heart
Listen with your ear

Many people need you
Many do not know
That what you carry in you
Is totally for show

Let the world hear you
Bump into a stranger
Oh, I'm sorry, are you ok?

Walk a little with him
Let him hear you speak
Tell him you had to share your smile today

You were just following your feet.

Remember to Give

If I could remember every thought
Every word that crossed my mind

I'd be a song writer
I'd be a poet
I'd be a millionaire

If I could remember all the names
Of all the faces of all the people
I've met

I'd have a lot of smiles to share
And names to remember
Of those I've not met yet

If I can remember, that in our hearts
We have so much love, we live

Would you not want the same for you
It's like our blood
It's in us to give!

What Day Beholds

What day beholds
The seconds tick
The minutes pass
The hours exceed the night

A good night's sleep
A resting space
A slip into a dream
A night to relax of peace and rest
A comfort to us all

Count the stars
Count the sheep
Count your fingers and toes

Count your blessings
Count your friends
And in your heart you'll know

Everything will be alright.

Love is (<3)

This is me
This is you

All that matters
Is what we do

Give a smile
Share a grin

Want nothing back
Hold nothing in!

See Us

See us in Your eyes
See us in Your heart
See us in Your thoughts
See us from the start

Teach us to be honest, humble
Loving and true

Love us, as we love You
Forgive us all the wrong we do

See us learn from our mistakes
See us fail, try again
And teach us all, what it takes

When the timing is right
And our hopes come true
Then we will be
In the arms of You.

Some of Me

Saskatchewan, to me, is fun
Where my dad grew up
I long to run

Port Coquitlam is in my past
I grew up there
It went by so fast

Ruskin came and went
Before I blew it, I sailed right through it
I was blessed with Mary
And I knew it

In Maple Ridge, we grew close together
She grew up so fast
Our love is forever

Later on, I met a man
He cares for me, loves me
Stands by me and married me

I am so blessed
My daughter grown
My husband is terrific

What I love most
The life I chose
Is blessed in knowing
Jesus is in it.

I Don't Know

I don't know a lot of things
Like politics and news
What I do know, is love and happiness
Is what it brings

I know about baking, art and music
About friends and how to make them

I don't know why others don't see it
When a person in need is easy to please

You become a friend, share your time
Share your thoughts to ease their pain
Loneliness will surely seize

Not knowing can leave your mind ready
For what your heart can bring

If I had a choice of knowing or love
The answer to me, is clear

Fill my heart with love to give
Happiness will stay near.

  Christine J. Logan

Why I Like What I Like

I don't know why I like what I like
But I like it

I like bugs and worms
Bats and snakes
Spiders, toads and cats

I like smiles and grins
Giggles and laughs
And being where it's at

I like when things go well
I like heights and trees
And all life's pleasant smells

I like to meet new people
I like to share my smile
I like to hear good music
And the option to turn the dial

But, most of all...
I just like what I like
Because I like it!

The Greatest Festival of Light

The greatest festival of light
Comes from within
Not from sight

The switch is within us
We have control
To turn it up high
Or way down low

This awesome light
We show to others
To brighten the way
And keep on track
To help each other see ahead
And not look back

This light we have inside us
Lights our way to guide us

See your goals
See your heart
See your way

Stay out of the dark.

Life's Mystery

Life is but a mystery
One step closer
For me to see

To see behind me
With one eye shut
To be able to speak
Without the "but"

I learn as I go
Try not to say no
Walk ever so gentle
Step on no toes

I don't know the future
I can only imagine
The closer I get
The less I fathom.

Wow!

Wow, so it goes
Beyond the space
No one knows

To each his own
Or so they say
Hard to believe life ends this way

Live it up, be very happy
Don't give in, be very sappy

We each know, our noses grow
When lies we tell are told

Hold your head up high and look ahead
You'll be surprised what unfolds

Love and truth will be your light
Take hold your heart
It'll be your sight.